The Beauty of Australia

THE
BEAUTY OF AUSTRALIA

Robin Smith

with text by

Osmar White

VIKING O'NEIL

Twelve Apostles, Port Campbell, Victoria

Waterways of the Great South Land

For well over a century travel writers have observed the convention of describing Australia, the Great South Land of ancient geographers, as a continent of infinite scenic subtlety which can be appreciated only by those patient and curious enough to endure climatic hardships and make long, monotonous journeys for the thrill of discovering oases. Australia, they claim, is a sombre land in which the shapes of nature are unfamiliar, the colours of verdancy muted, and the vistas depressingly vast. It is a land in which time is dimensionally different and silence and loneliness all-pervading.

No one who really knows Australia can accept this convention as logically founded. It grossly misrepresents both by overstatement and inaccurate generalisation. Australia has many faces, many moods, many climates. In the far north it is sub-equatorial, in the extreme south sub-antarctic. It has blazing deserts, but it also has rain-drenched jungles, snow-capped mountains, woodlands, moors, prairies and marshes. It has peaks which pierce the sky like needles, mesas, razorbacks, saw-tooth ranges ... rivers which meander placidly, rivers which race and roar in a series of cataracts all the way from their sources to the sea. And rivers which hide themselves underground for hundreds of kilometres, appearing only as still, limpid pools between sandbars.

It is surely absurd to assert that such a geographical cocktail never reveals the beauty of the earth obviously or intimately — that its many flavours are eternally blunted by a kind of romantic, antipodean *tristesse de distance*.

There are many parts of Australia which, even to the most unacclimated European eyes, are just as clearly beautiful as parts of Switzerland, Scandinavia, Great Britain or Greece — or of North America, Africa or Asia. The colours of the landscape are no more and no less subtle. The quality of the light is no less determined by season and latitude, and the forms of nature are no less familiar than the forms of nature in any other part of the world.

Buchan Point, North Queensland
View north to Ellis Beach and Port Douglas.

True, the Australian scene — or perhaps one should say the Australian scenic pageant — contains much that is unique. But in striving over-hard to isolate and represent this uniqueness, writers, and for that matter painters and photographers, have often lost sense of perspective and have detracted from, rather than added to, an understanding of the country they have attempted to portray.

The collection of camera studies in this book represents a rebellion from the convention of portraying Australia as a sad, brooding, perverse country for which one must first acquire a taste before coming to appreciate its quality. It is a collection which records the joyous rediscovery of familiar beauties — green grass, blue hills, bright flowers, calm waters, tall trees and sunshine which caresses rather than sears. Australia is no less bountifully endowed with all these things than the rest of the pleasantly habitable earth.

It is a fact of geography that Australia is the driest of the continents; but it is also a fact of geography that areas of the country larger than many European and Asian states never experience crippling drought. There are thousands of kilometres of rivers which never cease to flow and scores of lakes — both natural and man-made — serving populated districts where an abundance of water rather than a dearth of it determines the pattern of living.

Scores of clear, fast-flowing streams have their sources on the eastern watershed of the Great Dividing Range, a chain of mountains which extends for more than 3000 kilometres down the eastern seaboard where the mean annual rainfall is higher than in England's home counties and most of Western Europe.

When British colonists first established settlements on the central coast of New South Wales towards the end of the 18th century and set out to explore the hinterland, they at first followed the river valleys and were deeply impressed by the fertility and beauty of the coastal plains.

Governor Phillip, founder of Sydney, described the lower reaches of the Hawkesbury River where it enters the Pacific at Broken Bay as 'the finest

5

piece of water I ever saw'. Nearly a hundred years later Anthony Trollope, the famous English novelist and traveller, wrote that he found the same estuary 'more enchanting than either the Rhine or the Mississippi'.

Few who have cruised the myriad arms of Broken Bay with its densely wooded foreshores and expanses of silky water would complain that either Phillip or Trollope dealt in hyperbole, or that the enthusiasm they expressed for this lovely region would have been better justified if they had added some qualification to the effect that this gentle charm was, of course, far from typical of the whole continent!

The moods, the 'personalities', of Australia's east-flowing rivers, are excitingly varied. In the far north they are unmistakably tropical, subject to monsoonal flooding, and — particularly within the 'pocket' of hill jungle which extends along the seaward watershed of the Divide between Townsville and Cooktown — bear a marked resemblance to the streams which drain the highlands of the Malayan peninsula. The great Burdekin, too — torpid in the dry season and tumultuous in the wet — has Asian counterparts.

The scenic spectrum of the east Australian coast is wide — and given brilliance by a plethora of waterways. On the far side of the mountains the outlook is different and far more in accordance with traditional notions of what the countryside Down Under should look like. But here again rivers colour the complexion of nature.

The great Murray-Murrumbidgee system is fed by the run-off of copious rainfall on the Southern Highlands of New South Wales and by the melting of the winter snowfields of the Australian Alps. A traveller who followed the course of either stream from its headwaters in the Snowy Mountains to the point of confluence south-east of Mildura and from there followed through to the mouth of the Murray at Lake Alexandrina — in all a distance of more than 2000 kilometres — would observe a cross-section of temperate zone Australia more widely representative than that which could be provided by any other single inland journey.

The rivers rise in alpine heaths at an altitude of more than 1800 metres. For half the year these high plains are snow-mantled. Six hundred metres lower, their waters flow swiftly through deep, winding valleys between ridges blanked, or their upper slopes, by stands of bizarrely twisted snow-gums and by forests of huge eucalyptus trees at lower levels.

Then the terrain changes. The streams enter increasingly flat, dry country and meander through wheatlands and pastures, their banks thinly fringed with mighty red gums and weeping willows or breaking back into lagoons and swampy billabongs which are host to a clamorous population of waterfowl.

Here and there, like baroque gems strung along threads of tawny water, are patches of intensive cultivation sustained by irrigation from dams, barrages and locks built across the main streams and their tributaries.

Many of these artificial lakes are magnificent bodies of water, aquatic playgrounds for tens of thousands of Australians as well as the mainstay of important rural industries. Notable among them are the Hume reservoir near Albury and Lake Eildon, which impounds the Goulburn and Delatite Rivers, both Victorian tributaries of the Murray.

Water conservation has greatly changed the physical appearance of this part of the continent. The Murray, Murrumbidgee and Darling were once navigable by paddle steamers for an aggregate of thousands of kilometres, but their flow has been so greatly reduced by diversion for irrigation that nowadays only a few tourist boats ply on the deeper pools near Swan Hill and Echuca in Victoria or upstream from Lake Alexandrina in South Australia. Vistas of cropland, vineyard and orchard have replaced the landscape of primordial red-gum forest and arid savannah familiar to the pioneers of last century.

The environment familiar to most Australians is one created by sizeable rivers, lakes and reservoirs — and by the nearness of the sea. The continent has a coastline of 50 000 kilometres, more than the circumference of the earth, and much of it is boldly delineated and colourful.

In north-eastern Queensland, the Kimberley coasts of Western Australia, southern New South Wales, Victoria and Tasmania, mountain ranges between 1000 and 1500 metres high, plunge precipitously down to sea-level.

The Kimberley inlets and sounds and parts of the deeply indented seaboard of Tasmania are in their own ways as spectacular as the fiordlands of Norway or New Zealand. But these regions are remote and inaccessible and it is the gentler littoral of North Queensland which attracts hundreds of thousands of sightseers and holidaymakers every winter.

The tourists come to admire the superb coral gardens of the Great Barrier Reef which extends for 2500 kilometres from Torres Strait to the Tropic of Capricorn and is renowned throughout the world as an enthralling 'museum' of marine life. But when the travellers' expectations are transmuted into experience, it often turns out that their most enduring memories derive less from the wonders revealed in glass bottomed boats or underwater observatories than from the beauty of jewel-like islets and cays in fleckless seas of sapphire and emerald, looming blue headlands and peaks, and slim crescents of white sand over which tall palms lean and flame trees blaze. Night on the Great Barrier Reef is as enchanting as day. Fireflies dart in the pisonia thickets, phosphorescence runs on the tide and the stars seem near enough to touch. The only sounds to be heard are the susurration of the trade winds and the distance-muted thunder of the Pacific pressing its eternal assault on the coralling shield of the land. Nowhere is matchless scenery more concentrated than in the great, island-studded 'lagoon' between the reef and the Queensland coast.

South of the tropic the shore is abruptly transformed. The ocean gnaws at the body of the land itself and creates a series of sweeping golden beaches often backed by a belt of high sand dunes or salt marches and shallow sea-lakes.

This is the coast for sun-and-surf worshippers, with 1500 kilometres of hot sand segmented by tabular sandstone headlands, warm sea water, and mild winds for most of the year.

Still further south the mood of the coast changes yet again. The land ends more often in sheer cliffs which are not part of a truncated mountain spur but the abrupt slicing-off of a flat-topped, upthrust land-mass.

The ocean's sculpture of the continental bedrock on parts of the Victorian coast west of Port Phillip Bay is majestic, intricate and of gargantuan proportions. No seascapes could be more breathtakingly wild than those to be seen along Tasmania's west coast or in the Great Australian Bight where the mighty rollers born of Antarctic hurricanes destroy themselves in a foaming maelstrom at the base of a limestone escarpment of overhanging cliffs which stretches unbroken for more than 600 kilometres.

Enclosed waters at these high latitudes, particularly in Tasmania, bear a marked resemblance in summer to the narrows between the Baltic and the North Sea. The estuary of the Derwent and the bays protected by the Forestier and Tasman Peninsulas are ideal for boating and sailing. They are ringed by high, heavily wooded ranges and sheltered from prevailing winds and mountainous swells of the Southern Ocean. The number of Hobart citizens who own small pleasure craft and use them enthusiastically in the warm, calm season of long days between November and April is proportionately greater than in Sweden's capital, Stockholm.

Scandanavians and Tasmanians have in common a deep and abiding love of the sea. Both peoples live in an environment where they can indulge it under idyllic conditions.

*Porongorups Reservoir,
Western Australia*

Two notably beautiful mountain ranges
rise from the western escarpment of the
continent in the south-western corner
of W.A. They are the Porongorups and
the Stirling Range in the heart of the
karri forests for which the State is
famous. The rainfall of this region
averages between 1000 and 1500 millimetres a year and the countryside is
green for most of the time. But a
number of small water storages have
been built in the hills to supply small
farming and timber-milling towns on
the coastal plains. In spring the forest
floor is covered with a profusion of
brilliant wildflowers.

above: Bombo, Illawarra coast, New South Wales

The eastern seaboard of Australia south of Sydney offers magnificent panoramas. Occasional rocky outcrops, shaped by the pounding of the sea, interrupt the fine surf beaches that stretch along the beautiful craggy coastline. Dairy and mixed farms prosper in the climate which is mild and sunny except in the depth of winter, when big winds and seas sweep in from the Tasman.

right: The Archway, Port Campbell, Victoria

The coast west of Port Phillip Bay is rugged and majestic. Tremendous swells sweeping unbroken across the Southern Ocean from Antarctica have sculptured bold patterns in the cliffs. In the days of sail many fine ships were wrecked on the kelp-draped reefs which thrust far out to sea from the headlands. The heavily timbered Otway Ranges rise to the north of this savagely inhospitable shore.

above: Maingon Bay, from Tasman Island, Tasmania

The Tasman and Forestier Peninsulas south and east of Hobart are probably the most popular sight-seeing districts in the island State. On the ocean shore there are kilometres of towering cliffs and surf-washed skerries, and under the lee of the land a multitude of sheltered bays and beaches for bathing and fishing. New roads and walking tracks have now opened up this fascinating area to the tourist.

right: Charlesworth Bay, Coff's Harbour, New South Wales

A patchwork of forestry plantations, ploughed fields and orchards have replaced the dense red cedar forests which once clothed most of the North Coast of New South Wales. The climate is sub-tropical and excellently suited to the cultivation of bananas and other tropical fruit and vegetables for which the district is famous. However, valuable veneering timbers are still milled in the mountains and Coff's Harbour is the biggest timber port in Australia.

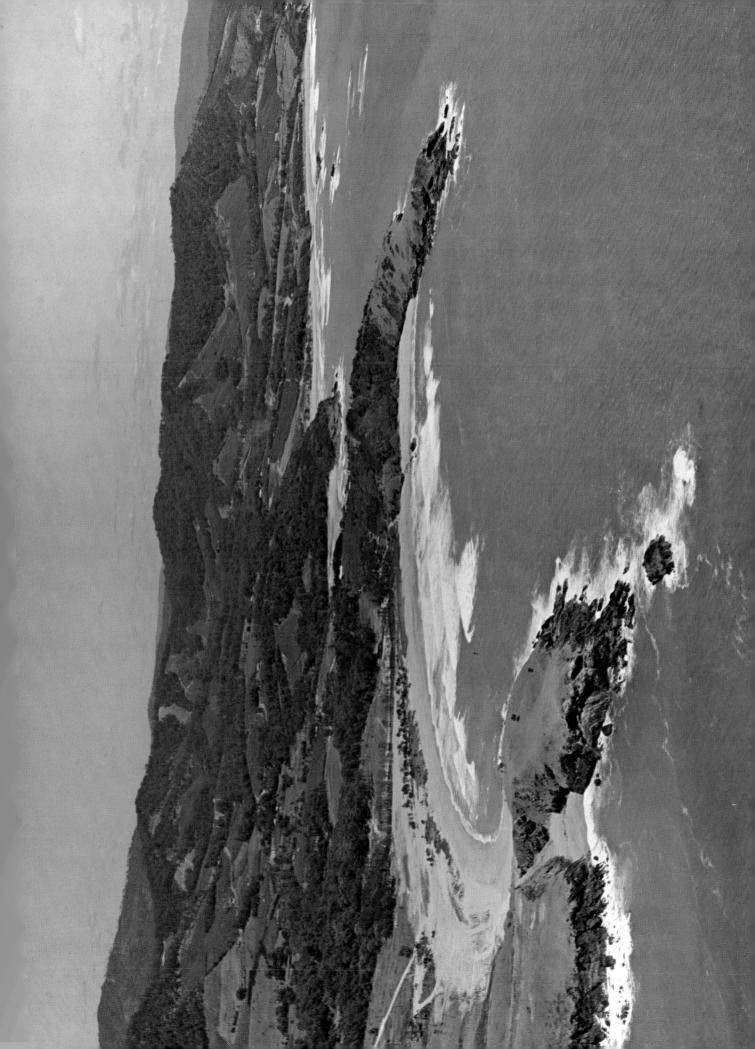

above: Daydream Island, Great Barrier Reef, Queensland

Many of the islands sheltered by the Great Barrier Reef along the Queensland coast have been developed as luxury holiday resorts and Daydream is among the most charming. It is a tiny islet only 3 kilometres long and around 100 metres wide. Accommodation units encircle a swimming pool and look across the spectacular Whitsunday Passage.

right: Bushy Cay, Great Barrier Reef, Queensland

The largest coral reef in the world extends 2000 kilometres from the mouth of the Fly River in Western Papua to Breaksea Spit east of the city of Gladstone. It is studded by innumerable cays and atolls formed by the breaking down of the dead coral into sand. This in time becomes compacted, rises above the surface of the sea and is clothed in vegetation germinated from wind and water borne seeds.

above: Lindeman Island, looking towards Pentacost Island, Queensland

Largest of the Cumberland Group in the Whitsunday Passage, 64 kilometres north of Mackay, Lindeman is a heavily timbered 'continental' island rising to a height of 200 metres at Mount Oldfield, from the summit of which 70 other Barrier Reef islands are visible. It has an area of about 800 hectares and has been declared a national park and wildlife sanctuary. Its bird and plant population is exceptionally diverse.

right: Dunk Island, Great Barrier Reef, Queensland

Dunk Island, a magnificent tropic isle 5 kilometres off the coast from Tully, is famed for its tranquility and unspoiled beauty. It has been developed as a major, high quality resort offering a range of accommodation units which vary in degrees of luxury, and were built such that they blend into the tropical surroundings. There are many graded walks through the island's superb rainforest.

above: Dunk Island, with Bedarra Island and Family Group in background

right: Surfer's Paradise, Gold Coast, Queensland

Between 1897 and 1923, Dunk Island was the home of the famous Australian writer 'Beachcomber' (E.J. Banfield) whose descriptions of its beauties have achieved the status of classical literature. The coral gardens of the reef off Dunk are exceptionally fine. The island is the largest of the Family Group, and has superb rainforest and scenery. More than 90 varieties of birds have been identified, and butterflies and wild orchids abound. The island once supported a sizeable population of Aborigines.

The flat, sandy coast of Queensland south of the Brisbane River has over the last 50 years been vigorously developed as an aquatic playground. Eighteen separate communities were fused by strip development and are administered as the City of the Gold Coast, the centre of which is Surfer's Paradise. Tens of millions of dollars have been invested in the construction of luxury hotels, a casino, apartments and amusement centres.

*above: Lindeman Island, looking towards
Pentacost Island, Queensland*

Largest of the Cumberland Group in the Whitsunday Passage, 64 kilometres north of Mackay, Lindeman is a heavily timbered 'continental' island rising to a height of 200 metres at Mount Oldfield, from the summit of which 70 other Barrier Reef islands are visible. It has an area of about 800 hectares and has been declared a national park and wildlife sanctuary. Its bird and plant population is exceptionally diverse.

*right: Dunk Island, Great Barrier Reef,
Queensland*

Dunk Island, a magnificent tropic isle 5 kilometres off the coast from Tully, is famed for its tranquility and unspoiled beauty. It has been developed as a major, high quality resort offering a range of accommodation units which vary in degrees of luxury, and were built such that they blend into the tropical surroundings. There are many graded walks through the island's superb rainforest.

above: Hayman Island, Great Barrier Reef,
Queensland

One of the most picturesque and intensively publi-
cised of tourist settlements among the Whitsunday
Group, Hayman Island is noted for its organised
and extensive entertainment, its high standard
accommodation, and for its beautiful island lagoon
which makes a perfect aquatic playground in front
of the Royal Hayman Hotel. There are walks to
lookouts, beaches and picnic spots, windsurfing,
scuba diving, tennis, archery and bowls, even a
betting shop and a secluded beachfront nightclub.

right: Green Island, Great Barrier Reef,
Queensland

A popular tourist attraction 27 kilometres north-
east of Cairns, Green Island is a true coral cay. The
island has an area of 13 hectares and is a marine
national park. It is surrounded by beautiful patches
of reef and crested with thick tropical vegetation.
Glass-bottomed boats and the underwater observ-
atory enable visitors to view the reef.

Coral Gardens of the Great Barrier Reef

The world's largest coral reef covers an area almost as large as that of Great Britain. It extends from Torres Strait down the Queensland coast to a point just south of the Tropic of Capricorn. This enormous mass of limy material, up to 120 metres thick and varying in width from 15 to 300 kilometres is composed entirely of the skeletons of coral polyps, minute marine animals with bodies about the size of pinheads. These tiny creatures form colonies of different sizes, shapes and colours according to their species.

Three hundred and fifty kinds of coral have now been identified on the Barrier — some of soft, gelatinous texture and some extremely hard and spiny. A specimem of soft coral growing on Hardy Reef is pictured top right. Bottom left is the exquisitely delicate *Pavona* which is prolific in the sheltered underwater grottoes of the Whitsunday Passage.

Both hard and soft varieties may be of any colour from pure white through pastel tints of yellow, green and red to intense purples and rich browns.

Some colonies are massive and complex in structure such as the heads of the *symphillial* and *porites* formations shown on the opposite page and harbour a variety of small marine animals and fish.

One of the most prolific and beautiful of the hard corals is *acropora acuminata* (staghorn coral) illustrated overleaf. Larger colonies may cover several hectares of reef foundation.

The greater part of the Barrier is permanently submerged, and can be viewed only from glass bottomed boats or by skin divers, but here and there horseshoe shaped platforms build up as the polyps die and deposit their skeletons. Parts of these rise above the surface or are exposed at low tide and it is on these elevated sections that sand and debris accumulated to form a cay spaced around a central lagoon.

Coral Gardens of the Great Barrier Reef

These lagoons, and the shallow shelves on the lee of the sheltering reef, support a rich flora of pastel tinted seaweeds in which mollusca of every imaginable variety, from giant clams weighing hundreds of kilograms to tiny cowries and conus, feed. Great schools of sunfish and other bright tropical species flash through this ever-moving submarine labyrinth.

Many kinds of decorative starfish also live in the coral and one species, *Acanthaster*, better known as The Crown of Thorns, has in recent years increased so rapidly that it reached plague proportions. It feeds only on living polyps and is now estimated to have killed about twenty per cent of the reef's coral.

Exactly what factors have contributed to the phenomenal increase in the Crown of Thorns has not yet been determined beyond doubt, but commercial fishing of a natural enemy, the giant Triton, for its decorative shell and pollution of inshore waters by sewage and leached agricultural fertiliser are suspect.

Unless nature itself decrees a natural remission of the pestilence or biologists can devise a practical means of control, the coral gardens of the Great Barrier Reef may perish entirely during the next quarter century.

above: Russell Falls, Mount Field National Park, Tasmania

Near the entrance to one of the most charming nature reserves in Southern Tasmania, the Russell River tumbles hundreds of metres in a series of filmy cascades through forests of tree-ferns (*Dicksonia antarctica*) and mossy declivities. The river drains forest land containing some of the world's largest trees, mountain ashes which in a nearby commercial forest concession attain a height of 98 metres. Specimens in the park top 87 metres.

right: Hunter River Landscape, New South Wales

About 160 kilometres north of Sydney, the valley of the Hunter River contains, besides enormous coal measures which have been exploited since the beginning of the nineteenth century, some of the richest agricultural and pastoral land in Australia. Cedar forests once covered these flats and rolling hills are given over to dairy farming, vineyards and market gardens. This peaceful scene near Scone is typical of the river's middle reaches.

above: Wannon Falls, Western District, Victoria

In a miniature Niagara particularly spectacular after heavy autumn and winter rains, the Wannon River makes its great leap forward to the sea near the Glenelg Highway north-west of the city of Hamilton. The river drains wide plains now mostly cleared of their open gum forests and developed into pastoral holdings which produce wool, fat lambs and prime cattle of outstanding quality.

right: Pearl Beach and Broken Bay, New South Wales

The magnficent Hawkesbury River enters the sea at Broken Bay nearly 20 kilometres north of Sydney. Quiet beaches, little coves and majestic unspoiled scenery between Broken Bay and Wisemans Ferry give the Hawkesbury its reputation for being the most beautiful river on the Australian continent.

Lake Eildon from Fraser National Park, Victoria

A vast inland lake framed in eucalypt forests, the Eildon reservoir impounds the waters of the Goulburn and Delatite Rivers, 140 kilometres north of Melbourne. The 130 square kilometre expanse of water is almost surrounded by the foothills of the Australian Alps and its 560 kilometres of foreshore have been re-afforested and developed to make it a magnificent aquatic playground. At holiday time it is crowded with launches, sailboats, canoes and fishermen whose hopes are often rewarded, because it and the streams which feed it are liberally stocked with trout and perch.

Peaks, Alpine Meadows and Tall Trees

Geographically Australia is the oldest of the continents and topographically the flattest. Only five per cent of its area of nearly 7 750 000 square kilometres has an altitude of more than 600 metres, and its highest mountain, Kosciusko, reaches a height of only 2227 metres. Yet, despite the geographers' undisputable statistics, the Great Dividing Range which runs inland from the eastern coast for 4000 kilometres contains some of the most rugged and beautiful mountain scenery in the world and some of the world's tallest forests.

In the far north the razorback ridges behind Cairns and Innisfail, jungle-clad to their crests, attain elevations of between 1200 and 1500 metres and are not superficially dissimilar to the foothills of the eastern Himalayas. The resemblance is underscored because tree species in the rainforest are related to those which grow in south and southeast Asian uplands, and the eucalypts which predominate over most of Australia are relatively scarce.

The mountains of North Queensland, unlike the Himalayan foothills, have no backdrop of mighty snow-peaks and glaciers, but they are split by enormous ravines through which monsoon-swollen streams race down to the sea in a series of turbulent waterfalls and rapids. At Wallaman Falls, near the little sugar milling town of Ingham, the Herbert River leaps over a 300-metre precipice of naked rock. The Tully and Millstream Falls on the Atherton Tableland are hardly less spectacular.

Hill country of a somewhat similar character is found far to the south along the Queensland-New South Wales border. Here again the ranges are cleft by fast-flowing rivers and blanketed by luxuriant vegetation.

Some of these tracts of virgin forest, in terrain so broken that it has repelled both timber-getters and land-takers, have been declared national parks. They are of particular interest to naturalists because, unlike forests in most other parts of Australia, they have never been swept by man-made fires.

From the high features of the McPherson Range and Lamington Plateau behind the Gold Coast

seaside resorts, from the summit of Mount Kaputar in the Nandewars and Point Lookout in the New England National Park, one may still see the woodlands of eastern Australia as they were before the coming of white men — a host of giant trees soaring above a rich green undergrowth of tree-ferns and saprophytic vines.

Even so these border forests lack something of the sylvan majesty which invests the big-timber country of Tasmania's Huon Valley or Victoria's Gippsland and Otway Ranges where the pale-trunked mountain ash (*Eucalyptus regnans*) vies with the Californian redwood for the distinction of being the tallest tree on earth.

Two small and geologically independent 'outriders' of the sub-tropical segment of the Great Divide are scenically notable — the Glass House Mountains just north of Brisbane and the Warrumbungles, about 160 kilometres west of the provincial city of Tamworth in northern New south Wales. Both are groups of massive trachyte pillars — the plugs of ancient volcanoes now starkly exposed by the crumbling of softer igneous rocks around them.

The tallest of the eleven peaks of the Glasshouse group is Beewah, a 550-metre pinnacle which shoots abruptly into the sky from an undulating plain which has in recent year been extensively cultivated to produce tropical fruit and vegetable crops.

The Warrumbungles, several hundred kilometres south and on the western watershed, are much larger and more varied in shape. They are the remnants of the rim of a gigantic volcano which exploded in Tertiary times — bluffs, domes, needles and crumbling sawteeth overtopped by the bulk of Exmouth and Crater Mountains. One extraordinary formation known as the Breadknife is 400 metres long, 90 metres high and only 9 metres thick at its base.

The valleys of the ruined crater provide a complex of microclimates which encourages an almost unbelievable diversity of plant and animal life. They are a kind of meeting place of species which have evolved on the arid inland plains, at

Wallaman Falls, near Inglam,
North Queensland

high altitudes, at sea level, on sandhills, or in swamps. Snow gums grow within 800 metres of sub-tropical fig trees and desert succulents almost alongside ground orchids and maidenhair ferns.

In central New South Wales, south of the summer rainfall zone, the scenery of the Great Dividing Range is radically altered. The mountain soils are less fertile and the annual range of temperatures greater. A much more sparse tree cover reveals the bold engraving of time on bedrock.

The deep valleys of the Blue Mountains are ringed by vertical sandstone cliffs in which rain, wind and frost have carved bizarre battlements. They are especially beautiful in late afternoon when the setting sun gilds the tawny rock faces and the base of cumulus clouds building up over the coastal plain.

The Blue Mountains barred exploration of the interior for a quarter century after the founding of Sydney. They were not conquered until 1813 when a ridge-top route across them was discovered by the explorers Blaxland, Wentworth and Lawson. They received their name because of the intense cobalt haze which tinted the distant bush — a phenomenon ingeniously explained by early observers who advanced the theory that it was caused by the diffraction of light by microscopic droplets of eucalyptus oil transpired by the gum forests. Conservative naturalists consider this explanation fanciful, but the fact remains that the Blue Mountains have become considerably less blue over the last thirty or forty years. The bleaching of the once brilliant colour has followed on a series of disastrous bushfires in the Jamieson, Grose and Megalong Valleys. Much of the tall timber was destroyed or severely damaged and has not yet regenerated.

South of the sandstone plateaus of the Blue Mountains the main range thickens and rises again to elevations of more than 1500 metres and the vegetation on the tops assumes an alpine or sub-alpine character. There are numerous intrusions of plutonic rocks in the tumbled sedimentary strata.

The highest mountains in the Australian Alps

as this part of the Divide has been called, are massive domes of granite thrusting up from deeply eroded tablelands. Kosciusko, Townsend, Twynham and the Ram's head Range all top 2130 metres.

At these latitudes the winter snowline descends to about 1500 metres and the whole range is thickly blanketed from June to September. Between 1200 and 1800 metres the ridges are often clothed with thickets of snow-gum (*E. coriacea*), scrubby little trees with fantastically twisted trunks and branches with white bark mottled and streaked in bright reds, browns and yellows. They are the antipodean counterpart of the conifers of high country in the northern hemisphere, and they are seen at their best after frost has encased them in a glittering filagree of ice.

Above the snow-gum line is a region of boggy heath and alpine meadows which blaze with flowers in early summer. Below the snow-gums sombre forests of ash, candlewood, ironbark and stringybark take over the mountainsides.

The winter snowfields of the Australian Alps have an area of 5000 square kilometres — more good ski-ing country than there is in the whole of Switzerland, but the season is short and the beginning and end of it unpredictable.

Personally I have never felt that the term 'Alps' is particularly apt as a designation for these mountains, however technically correct it may be. They have a magnificent solidity and their peaks command superb views, but they do not resemble the alps of Europe or New Zealand. A much closer scenic relationship can be observed in the mountains of Tasmania where the peaks soar, and crags and rocky ramparts are reflected in innumerable lagoons and tarns, and in lakes as clear, deep and still as Como or the Konigsee. The mountain lover who makes the four-day walk across Lake St Clair National Park before the high snows have melted will make a tour as authentically and invigoratingly alpine as any that could be made in Europe.

Cradle Mountain, Federation Peak, Frenchman's Cap — the bluffs and towers of the Hartz and Arthur Ranges — have a quality of majesty unimpaired by comparison with alpine scenery in any other part of the world. The summer flowers which bloom in the meadows at their feet match or surpass in variety and profusion those which spangle Tyrolean pastures in May — great fields of yellow and white daisies, anemones, buttercups, crimson bell-heaths, sun orchids, hopbush, bottle-brush and wild violets.

The rainforest flora of Tasmania contains several prolific species which do not occur on the mainland. Notable among these is the Antarctic beech, a gnarled, hairy tree with a spreading canopy of heavy green foliage. It also grows in parts of New Guinea, New Caledonia, New Zealand and South America. Its fossilised pollen has been found in the coal measures of Antarctica and supports the theory of some geologists that these regions were once coher-ent parts of a great land mass which stretched from the equator to the South Pole.

Tasmanian scrublands carry vegetation of unparal-leled density. Not even Amazonian jungles are more impenetrable. Large areas are covered by the notorious 'horizontal' (anodopetalum) which grows in stands so matted and tough that paths through it can be cut only by skilled axemen or, these days, by prospectors equipped with portable power saws.

A road was driven into the heart of Tasmania's south-western mountains to supply the workforce engaged on building dams on the Gordon River for hydro-electric power stations. In clear weather the drive from the little township of Maydena on the rim of the Derwent Valley to Lake Pedder is unforgettable. The highway slices through forests of beech, leatherwood, sassafras, hoop pine and gum, and crosses ridges which command tremendous panoramas of upland wilderness.

The Great Dividing Range and its long severed arm in Tasmania comprise the backbone of the world's flattest continent but it is by no means the only lofty mountain system in Australia. The huge ranges which rise in the central deserts are described in another section of this book, but there are many smaller areas of high country which are scenically notable.

The isolated Grampians of western Victoria are wild, bold and austere, and from their peaks and jutting bluffs of weathered sandstone, the climber can look out over some of south-east Australia's finest sheep pastures.

Beyond them, far to the north-west are the charming Mount Lofty Ranges with their feet in the rich farm lands and vineyards on the eastern shores of the Gulf of St Vincent. They are the playground and refuge from summer heat of the people of Adelaide. Their northward extension becomes the Flinders Ranges which, though they thrust deep into the waterless salt-lakes plains around Lakes Torrens, Eyre and Frome, can hardly be classed as mountains of the desert because they carry a heavy vegetation of river gums, casuarinas, native pines and acacias in valleys which are clothed in a chromatic splendour of wildflowers every spring.

In Western Australia, a high, rugged escarpment runs parallel to the coast for many hundreds of kilometres and traps rain borne on ocean winds in much the same way as the Great Dividing Range does in the east. Luxuriant forests of karri and jarrah grow in the south-west corner of the State.

The karri is a tree only slightly smaller than the mountain ash of the east and the biggest reach a height of neary 90 metres in valleys where the annual rainfall averages 1000 millimetres.

The Porongorups and the Stirling Range rise from the heart of the karri country and are a paradise for botanists because they abound in plant species which will not acclimatise in any other part of Australia or the world. They are in the most literal sense of the term, an exclusive garden of strange flowers and shrubs.

A journey through this exquisite bushland in spring, when the brown boronia perfumes the air and the clematis, hardenbergia and piercingly blue lechenaultia splash colour through the glades, is a journey never to be forgotten.

Bunyeroo Valley, Flinders Ranges, South Australia

Most accessible of Australia's desert mountains, the
Flinders Ranges are the northern sector of a
gigantic, shattering 'crease' in the earth's crust
which appeared in Tertiary times. The tops of the
ridges are bare and jagged, but the valleys carry a
scattering of hardy trees like this native pine and a
lush herbage after rain. The most well-known
feature in the entire Flinders Ranges is Wilpena
Pound, a huge plateau encircled by sheer cliffs.
Nearby is the beautiful Bunyeroo Valley, one of the
most spectacular in the Ranges.

above: Dove Lake, Cradle Mountain, Tasmania

The Cradle Mountain-Lake St Clair National Park of 1360 square kilometres is the largest scenic and wildlife reserve in Tasmania and it contains much of the State's most impressive alpine scenery. The jagged peaks and tors, at the foot of which are many beautiful small lakes and tarns, are deeply covered by snow in winter and covered by superb wildflowers in summer. The park is traversed by a walking track along which alpine huts are spaced.

right: Point Bonney, Flinders Ranges, South Australia

In coloration and atmosphere the Flinders Ranges are highly individual — layers of tan rock overlying shale beds of deep purple. The play of light on the arid peaks and through the valleys is endlessly fascinating. This country is at its best from July through September when the onset of summer with its fierce heat and northerly winds begins to wither the ground's cover of ephemeral grasses and flowering shrubs.

over: St. Mary's Peak (1170 metres), Flinders Ranges

*left: The Three Sisters, Blue Mountains,
New South Wales*

These remarkable towers of weathered sandstone
rise more than 450 metres above their talus slopes in
the Jamieson Valley, near Katoomba, 96 kilometres
west of Sydney. Here the setting sun gilds the
normally grey-and-ochre cliffs and mutes the
intense cobalt blue haze which gave this rugged
sector of the Great Dividing Range its name. It took
the first settlers quarter of a century to find a way
over these ramparts to the western plains.

*above: The McPherson Range from Lamington
Plateau, Queensland*

In the hinterland of Queensland's famous complex
of pleasure resorts, the Gold Coast, the McPherson
Range rise to an altitude of more than 1200 metres
and are covered by thick, sub-tropical forests which
have never yet been damaged by severe bushfires.
They contain many vivid flowering trees and host
more than 20 species of tree and rock orchids. The
deep canyons cut by mountain streams have many
spectacular caves and waterfalls.

above: Coonoowrin and Beerwah, Glasshouse Mountains, Queensland

These dramatically precipitous trachyte peaks, the plugs of ancient volcanoes, are located in a group of 11 about 64 kilometres north of Brisbane. They were sighted by Captain James Cook when he was sailing up the coast in 1770, and named by him because they reminded him of the glass furnaces of his native Yorkshire. Beerwah, the tallest spire, is 556 metres high.

right: Balconies Formation, The Grampians, Victoria

Wind and water have weathered the tilted sand-stone slabs of the Grampian mountains into strange shapes many of which project over dizzy drops into the valley below. The isolated range beyond the western end of the Great Divide is inclined at an angle of 30 degrees to the horizontal and the upper end of the massif is characterised by bold bluffs from which a tremendous panoramic view may be admired.

Mountain Contrasts

above left: Mount Feathertop, giant of the Victorian Alps, as seen from Mount Hotham (1862 metres).
below: View from Evans Lookout, near Blackheath, Blue Mountains. Sunset dips the savage cliffs in molten gold. In the deep shadows are concealed the finest blue-gum forests in Australia, protected from fire by the narrowness of the gorge, its inaccessibility, and high rainfall.

above: Wilson's Promontory.
View from Mount Oberon

A wild, desolate headland thrusting deep into the waters of Bass Strait, Wilson's Promontory has been reserved as a national park and sanctuary since 1908. Its highest point is Mount Latrobe, 742 metres above sea-level, which like many other peaks on its rocky spine, commands breathtaking views of coast and heathland; and of the tea-tree and lillipilli forests which flourish in the more sheltered valleys.

above: Skiers, Thredbo Valley, New South Wales

The high plains and peaks of the Australian Alps are thickly blanketed by snow from June to October in normal years and are a magnificent playground for winter sports enthusiasts. Ski-ing is now a fashionable sport and many clubs have built lodges which imitate Swiss mountain architecture. The effect is picturesque in snow time — not so happy when drifts have melted.

right: Threadbo Alpine Vallage

Snowfalls of one and two metres and drifts up to 9 metres are not uncommon in the blizzards which occasionally sweep the Alps. Note the snowgums and other small eucalypts which cover the ridge behind the lodges. They are the antipodean equivalent of the evergreen fir, spruce and pine trees which grow in European mountains. At higher altitudes their trunks and limbs are often twisted into bizarre shapes by the wind.

above: Mount Townsend, Snowy Mountains, New South Wales

These gorge-cleft highlands clothed in sombre forests are the great rain trap in which the Murray-Murrumbidgee river system has its source. An elaborate series of dams at lower levels harnesses the water-power to generate electricity for the big cities of Sydney and Melbourne, and feeds the canals of the Riverina irrigation system which contributes much to the rural wealth of the nation.

right: Peaks of Lyell, West Coast, Tasmania

Rarely indeed is a man-made desert beautiful, but the miracle has happened near Queenstown, a copper mining centre on Tasmania's wild west coast. Timber-getters stripped the hills of trees to feed the furnaces of the smelters, and chemical fumes from their stacks killed off any undergrowth remaining. The extraordinary range of colours reflected from the naked rock derives from mineral leaching.

Wilderness Tamed by Axe and Fire

It is a cliche frequently repeated in Australia that the pioneers who founded the nation tamed a savagely hostile land. Like most cliches, it is only partly true.

Australia was a physically difficult country to settle when the first fleet sailed into Port Jackson in 1778 and Governor Phillip raised the Union Jack on the shores of Farm Cove. Most of the countryside was thickly clothed in a type of vegetation which Europeans found depressing because it was different from what they were used to. Soils were recalcitrant. Game of a type which Europeans knew to be edible was non-existent. The fish in the rivers and sea were unfamiliar and hard to catch until their habits had been observed.

When promised supply-ships did not arrive at the expected time, Phillip and his soldiers and convicts very nearly starved.

Learning the tricks of making the country support its new settlers in basic food stuffs was a first priority. With axe and saw and fire, the first generation of pioneers set about demolishing the coastal forests with ferocious energy — clearing the land for the plough so that grain could be grown and sheep and cattle pastures established. This formula for 'development' was to be followed for the next one hundred and fifty years. The philosophy of the Australian land-takers was: 'If it is a tree that grows on ground where sheep and cattle can feed, then cut it down. If it is an animal that has not been domesticated for human use, then shoot it'.

Thus predatory man exterminated most of the coastal forests along the eastern and south-eastern coasts and very nearly exterminated its fauna. That many species of birds and animals peculiar to the region continue to survive is due to the fact that they have had mountain sanctuaries to which to retreat — terrain so rough and broken and infertile that the farmer or grazier would find no conceivable profit in clearing and fencing it.

The altered face of eastern Australia is, however, far from uncomely. In the far north the flats which once sustained great stands of native pines, ever-green 'oaks' and 'walnuts' and 'maples' allied to South-East Asian species have been transformed into a patchwork quilt of cultivation reminiscent of Java or the delta of the Mekong.

Much farther south, land on which gloomy cypress and drab stringybark grew now produces oil-seed crops, maize, tropical fruits and lucerne.

The human conquest of a wilderness does not necessarily substitute ugliness for beauty. Frequently the reverse is true. All in all the thin, green rind of Australia is today much more pleasing to European eyes than it was in the days when kangaroos left their tracks on the surf beaches.

The changes wrought by settlement of a land which was to all intents and purposes uninhabited were simply those which follow the clearing of forests for the cultivation of crops and pastures by traditional European methods.

When Phillip landed at Sydney Cove, the strip of mainly fertile well-watered land, varying in width between 50 and 500 kilometres which stretched for 4000 kilometres along the eastern and southern water-sheds of the Divide, was heavily wooded with eucalypts 'diluted' in the river valleys north of Sydney by cedars, various pines and — in the far north — by species related to those found in South East Asia.

One hundred and fifty years later these forests had vanished and been replaced by a ragged green ribbon of farms producing all sorts of crops from sugar cane and tropical fruit to oats and potatoes.

Inevitably the physical appearance of the country was greatly altered, tamed, by this intensive utilisation of the soil. The surviving gums still scrawled the Australian signature across the landscape, but there were many areas where the willows, poplars, elms and oaks introduced by settlers as shade and shelter trees became scenically dominant.

'Europeanisation' of the countryside is most marked, of course, in the cooler latitudes — on the South Coast of New South Wales, in Victoria and Tasmania. Entire districts have taken on a likeness of rural England, with rivers and brooks flanked by perenially green fields and fringed by plantations and hedgerows which blossom ethereally in spring. Axe, plough and harrow have created a gentle world, as traditionally rustic as the English downs — a world of rounded contours, verdant fields and plantations which are rich with glowing colour when the first frosts come in autumn.

The most dramatic and beautiful examples of contrived environmental change are probably to be found in southern Tasmania, along the Derwent Valley where deciduous trees have acclimatised particularly well and thousands of hectares are devoted to the cultivation of apples, pears and hops; and along the Upper Murray where the river traverses the lower foothills of the Alps. Here each tributary creek is bordered by century-old willows and poplars and weathered farm buildings dream in the shade cast by cypresses, pin-oaks, peppercorns and walnuts.

Save for an occasional smoke or dust haze above the sullen, blue smudge of distant mountains, there is little in the prospect of the Upper Murray to suggest the Australia of popular legend — the implacably hostile, enigmatic country in which climatic violence has bred a race of men innured to violent fluctuations of fortune. The region is no more resistant to settlement by Caucasians than Southern France, Italy, Greece or Spain. Its affinity with those countries is, indeed, reflected in the ease with which it is now being populated by migrants from southern Europe who take up land and grow fruit, vegetables, tobacco and mixed farm produce with less toil and considerably more profit than they could at home.

Farther west the mixed farming country gives place to grainlands and sheep pastures — a mosaic of ploughed earth, growing crops and bleached stubble according to the season; and in the huge tracts of country now under irrigation, of vineyards, orange groves and stone-fruit orchards. Ricefields extend over many thousands of hectares of what was, before the water was brought to it, a parched, dun-coloured plain covered thinly by native grasses and clumps of stunted eucalypts.

Much of the dry savannah land on the gradually sloping western side of the Divide has also undergone a pleasant transformation since the first squatters drove their flocks and herds through the mountain passes from the coast. Exotic trees are much less evident, but fine specimens of native box, woollybutt, kurrajongs and pines have been preserved for stock shelter and the less decorative scrub cleared to make place for introduced pasture plants.

A belt of improved grassland now extends inland from the watershed for upwards of 250 kilometres, from the Queensland-New South Wales border into western Victoria. It is tranquil country — spacious, uncluttered and highly individual because the European 'graft' which was successful elsewhere at temperate latitudes did not take here. It is 'the wide brown country' of the lyric Australian poets —certainly with its cycles of drought and flood, heat and cold, scarcity and plenty neither more nor less marked than similar cycles on the prairies of the United States or the steppes of Asia. In the conception of a vast majority of Australians it is 'the bush' or 'the country', as distinct from the Outback or the Never Never. It was here that the Swagman camped down by the billabong and the Squatter was mounted on his thoroughbred . . . rural, in its own inimitable way, not feral.

This aspect of Australia is, I think, best seen in the eastern Riverina, the plains at the foot of the New England tablelands, and the Darling Downs — districts in which cultivation has added charm to expression of nature.

Human agency has not altered inhabited parts of the tropical coast to quite the same degree as it has the south east. The sugar farming strip between Townsville and Cairns, once smothered in jungle, now resembles the intensively farmed plains of West Java, particularly from the air. Asian and other exotic flowering species have established themselves in the settlements and from September onward to the breaking of the monsoon daub the streets with improbably violent reds, purples and yellows. The evening air carries all the familiar perfumes of both eastern and western equatorial zones — frangipanni, magnolia, jasmine, hibiscus, tree-tulip and wild ginger. Palms from the Indies, the Americas and Oceania, rain trees from Sumatra, banyans from Madras have blended unobtrusively with the vegetation natural to the region. In the high rainfall areas of North Queensland there seems less botanical incongruity when a breadfruit tree towers above a treefern glade than there is in the south when a mighty elm rears its head over the redgums lining some billabong.

I have written that Australia has many faces, many moods, Of these, the most familiar are gentle.

above: Pineapple Plantation, Nambour, Queensland

Rich volcanic soils and liberal rainfall make the coastal plain of central and southern Queensland ideal for the cultivation of tropical fruit and vegetables. Pineapples, bananas, ginger, macadamea nuts and — strangely — high quality strawberries are cropped around Nambour, a small town which is regarded as the 'capital' of an attractive district now promoting itself as The Sunshine Coast.

right: Showground and Racecourse Approach, Tumut, New South Wales

This magnificent show of elms is at the entrance of the Tumut showground and racecourse. A brisk mountain climate enables these deciduous trees to flourish and autumn brings many visitors with cameras to record this superb avenue.

Forest Sunset, Pemberton, Western Australia

above left: Cattle Droving, Upper Hunter River, New South Wales

The breeding of prime beef cattle is an increasingly important industry in many coastal districts of eastern Australia. Some of the finest stud farms are located in the rich tributary valley of the Upper Hunter where climate and pastures are ideal and markets not too far distant.

left: Ruins at Highfield Estate, near Stanley, Tasmania

One of the first convict settlements in northern Tasmania was established in the early 1800s near Stanley, a small fishing village under the lee of The Nut, a table-topped headland projecting into Bass Strait. The stone buildings are excellent examples of the stonemason's craft, but many of them are now crumbling and Tasmanians with an interest in preserving the historic relics of their State are moving to restore them.

above: Pioneer Valley, near Eungella, Queensland

Rich cane and fruit farms have been established on the river flats 80 kilometres west of Mackay, sugar capital of Central Queensland. The Pioneer River drains Eungella National Park, largest mountain reserve in the State. The valley is traversed by a fine scenic road on which Sky Window Walk is a notable and appropriately named vantage point.

above: Richmond Bridge, Southern Tasmania

This beautiful freestone bridge about 25 kilometres from Hobart on the road to Port Arthur was designed by David Lambe and built by convicts in 1823. It is the oldest structure of its kind still in use in Australia. Local stone quarried at Butcher's Hill was used, but formidable engineering problems — the river floods violently — raised the cost of construction to £20,000, an almost astronomical figure for bridge work in those days.

right: Mount Warning, Tweed River District, New South Wales

Some of the gentlest and most classically pastoral scenery in Australia is to be found on the border of Queensland and New South Wales, some 110 kilometres south of Brisbane. Chief industries of this district are sugar and tropical fruit growing on farms originally cut out of the forest. But some valuable timber is still to be found in the mist filled valleys of the ranges.

above: Mount Abrupt, the Grampians, Victoria

Bold promontories thrusting out into an ocean of grass, Mount Abrupt and its sister peak, Mount Sturgeon (lower slopes in middle distance) are typical of the marginal bluffs of this isolated range in which many of the important rivers of the State's western district have their headwaters.

above right: Goulburn Valley Billabong, Central Victoria

The Goulburn River, a tributary of the Murray which it joins near Echuca, drains a wide, fertile valley in which a prosperous fruit growing industry has been established. The flats are studded with quiet lagoons and backwaters frequented by a host of waterfowl.

right: Wildflowers of the West

Eighty per cent of the 6 000 flowering plants species listed by botanists in Western Australia occur nowhere else on the continent. Many of them are unique in form and brilliance of colour. No wonder thousands of tourists flock to Perth in spring to enjoy a wonderland of floral beauty, sunshine and singing birds.

above left: Sheep pastures, Stirling Range, Western Australia

From some aspects the Stirling Ranges of Australia's far south-west bear a marked resemblance to Victoria's Grampians. Both regions are rich in wild-flowers and both dominate lowlands which support high-quality flocks on scientifically improved pastures.

left: Hereford herd, Mary River, Central Queensland

Coal, sugar, timber and dairy produce account for much of the wealth of the Wide Bay district of Queensland, but in recent years greater emphasis has been given beef production with the opening up of the wallum gum country behind the coastal strip. Trace elements added to chemical fertilisers have greatly increased carrying capacity.

above: Buring off sugar cane near Innisfail, North Queensland

When Australian sugar cane crops are mature, the leaves are burned off to facilitate the operation of giant mechanical harvesters. The glow of cane fires at night and a dence haze of blue smoke overhanging the countryside by day are features of the coastal landscape in late spring.

above: Sunrise, Maria Island, Tasmania

Silky calm waters, subtle colouring and intricate tree silhouettes are typical of Tasmania's sheltered east coast. Maria Island lies north of the Tasman and Forestier Peninsulas 8 kilometres from the popular holiday resort of Triabunna on the Tasman Highway between Hobart and Launceston.

right: Bushfire in the karri forest, Western Australia

Fires — mostly caused by human agency — sweep through the heavily timbered country south of Perth with tragic regularity. They are incredibly destructive but have their moments of melancholy beauty as this study of a sorely wounded forest shows.

above: Woodland Track, Mount Macedon, Victoria

An extinct volcano 1013 metres high and 61 kilometres north-west of Melbourne, Mount Macedon is a fashionable residential area. On Ash Wednesday 1983, bushfires that were among the worst this country has known, destroyed about half of the beautiful gardens and nurseries in the Macedon area. However the rich soil, high elevation and copious rainfall have hastened the rebuilding process.

right: Giant karri trees, Porongorups, Western Australia

Eucalyptus diversicolor (karri) vies with *Eucalyptus regnans* (mountain ash) for the distinction of being the tallest growing tree in the southern hemisphere. Its straight white trunk can rise to a height of more than 45 metres before producing branches. The relative sparseness of forest undercover in the karri country enables observers to appreciate the symmetry and majesty of these giants.

above: Hunter River landscape, east of Scone, New South Wales

Fields of muted green, soft blue skies and rolling foothills on the horizon are characteristic of these spacious uplands in spring and summer. But heavy autumn and winter rains transform a deceptively gentle stream into an angry river which can break its banks and inundate hundreds of thousands of hectares of farms, vineyards and orchards. Flooding is a major problem along all northern rivers.

right: Salvation Jane in flower, South Australia

One of the most spectacular of the dry country ephemerals below the tropics, this plant — regarded as a noxious weed in other States because it is poisonous to stock — makes a brilliant display on the park-like savannahs of the Flinders Range. In different seasonal conditions the same slopes may be blanketed with wild hops, parakeelya or golden everlastings.

over: Morning Mists in the Forest, Porongorups, Western Australia

above: Golden or Broad-leafed Wattle, Queensland

More than 600 different varieties of wattles - members of the Mimosa family of the Acacia genus — have been classified on the Australian mainland. Of these the golden or broad leafed wattle (the national floral emblem) is widely distributed in Queensland. Its dense clusters of bright yellow blossom blaze gaily through the more open forest lands of the foothills in late winter.

right: Purlingbrook Falls, Springbrook,
Southern Queensland

Many of the crystal clear rivers rising on the Lamington Plateau of the McPherson Range race down to the Pacific Ocean in a series of filmy waterfalls. Purlingbrook Falls, with their deep viridian pool and jungle-covered amphitheatre where many arboreal orchids flower, are one of the most delightful picnic spots in the great Lamington Plateau National Park.

above: Lindsay Park, Angaston, South Australia

The Angaston district of the Barossa Valley 50 kilometres north-east of Adelaide is famous for its vineyards and the excellence of its table and dessert wines. On the eastern watershed of the Gawler Ranges, the region enjoys a magnificent climate and, besides grapes, produces olives and stud cattle and horses. Evidence of its prosperity is given by the many fine old homesteads sited to command lovely views of mountains and river.

right: Koala's Dinner

Soft grey and white fur, bright shoe-button eyes and a sleepy disposition make the koala (whose official name is *Phasocolarctus cinereus*) one of the best loved animals in the world. This little marsupial, which has difficulty acclimatizing outside Australia, has one of the most specialized diets of any mammal. It thrives only on leaves from certain varieties of gum trees — about ten in all.

Cities in Search of
the Best in Two Worlds

Four out of five Australians live in cities or large provincial towns built on or near the coast. In the sociological sense they are as urbanised as the people who live in England's Midlands or the seaboard cities of the United States and are almost totally dissociated from the rural environment.

It is true, however, that Australian city-dwellers enjoy advantages in living conditions not generally shared by urban populations in most other parts of the world.

For a start, gross overcrowding is extremely rare and confined to a few run-down areas in Sydney and Melbourne where re-housing has lagged behind a rapidly increasing demand for inner suburban accommodation. Slums of the sort that blight New York, Los Angeles, London, Rome or Naples do not exist in Australia.

This is in part due to economic prosperity of a high order and to the abundance of peripheral land available for metropolitan expansion; but climate and favourable terrain are extremely important factors. The founders of Australia's cities were not inhibited by military or political considerations when they chose the sites on which to build. They came to an enormous country at the ends of the earth inhabited only sparsely by nomadic primitives whose dispossession from their tribal hunting grounds could hardly be rated as conquest.

On the whole the first settlers chose well. They established themselves in localities where there was virtually unlimited room for expansion and where the surrounding countryside was both arable and beautiful.

The physical and climatic qualities of their setting dominate all the State capitals and determine to a very large degree their aesthetic character and liveability, for it is nature rather than art which makes them pleasant cities.

Sydney's magic is compounded of three elements: its magnificent harbour, the broken rocky land over which it has grown back from the waterfront

left: Central business district, Perth

and a mysterious phenomenon which I think is best described as South Pacific light; and best observed from the harbour on a calm morning in spring or early summer. No one who has seen the foreshores of Port Jackson under such conditions would debate the proud Sydneysiders' boast that they live beside one of the loveliest sheets of water in the world. Architectural vandalism — and a good deal of it has been perpetrated in Sydney in recent years — cannot destroy the impression that a city so caught between sea and sky and so gently kissed by the sun *must* be a beautiful place to live in.

The second city of the Commonwealth, Melbourne, is not so well endowed scenically. It grew from a nucleus of about one square kilometre of carefully selected and surveyed land in relatively flat country near the mouth of the Yarra River at the head of Port Phillip Bay — a large almost land-locked inlet with sandy or marshy foreshores and none of Port Jackson's noble sandstone headlands and deeply recessed bays.

It did, however, enjoy certain advantages over Sydney. The level terrain allowed it to expand in an orderly pattern and its cooler climate and richer soil favoured the acclimatisation of deciduous trees and shrubs from the northern hemisphere.

Thus Sydney as it matured retained an antipodean individuality bounded by its rocky, scrub-covered ridges and ocean beaches pounded by the Pacific surf; and Melbourne developed its 'English' character from parks, gardens and street plantations in which European species virtually ousted native evergreens.

Nevertheless, the enthusiasm with which the first two generations of Melbournians set about re-creating a little bit of old England on the banks of the Yarra had happy results. Truly magnificent public domains were established in wastelands on the margins of the original settlement and a community tradition of tree-planting and flower-gardening was established and is respected to the present day. Melbourne is a strikingly handsome city in the season when the first roses are in bloom and when the noble elms and oaks and birches have put out new leaves; it is a colourful city when autumn is turning to winter; and it is a city of sombre dignity when branches are bare and a golden sunset undercuts rainclouds driven by the easterly gales of June and July. Sydney somehow manages to retain its gay and sometimes rather raffish prettiness the whole year round.

Both cities can only be described as architecturally undistinguished and inconsistent. Their growth has been phenomenally rapid and therefore largely unplanned. Early public buildings were designed in simple Georgian and Colonial styles, often by talented emancipist architects, and built in local stone by master masons. Some were preserved and confer elegance on short sections of old thoroughfares. But most were obliterated in the welter of ornate Victoriana in which well-to-do merchants indulged after the gold rushes swelled the population and put the country on its feet economically.

Until the 1950s Australian cities somewhat resembled English provincial towns in the architectural style of their 'downtown' areas. Their residential suburbs crept steadily outward from the commercial and industrial nucleus, an ever-spreading, amorphous mass of brick and timber villas, each set in its own fenced plot and built to whatever design was currently fashionable in low cost housing.

This uncontrolled sprawl — the low density of urban population — created formidable civic difficulties. It substantially increased the cost of providing public utilities and eventually inflated land prices in desirable areas to absurd levels. But it undeniably conferred on urban Australians unusual privileges — domestic privacy unknown to dwellers in cities where most of the population are accommodated in terrace housing, apartments or tenaments, and the opportunity to express individuality in many ways ordinarily open only to countrymen.

In the big cities of the east, however, there are signs which indicate that this golden age of residential permissiveness is coming to an end. The hope that decentralization would accompany population increase has not been realised in any substantial way and Sydney and Melbourne are going through an alarming phase of re-development in which older buildings, good and bad alike, are being demolished and replaced by multi-storey office blocks and apartments, the designers of which have been strongly influenced by American architects of the 1940s and 1950s. No one can yet say how much the visual — and perhaps social — character of the cities will be altered by the advent of the glass steel and concrete skyscraper and the high-rise flat building. Low density suburbia, masked in Melbourne at least by plantations and shrub-

beries, will probably endure for a few decades yet.

The smaller State capitals — particularly Hobart, Adelaide and Perth — are as yet not large enough to have developed aesthetic complexities. They are consistent, compact and clearly dominated by their environment.

Hobart, on the western bank of the scenically superb Derwent estuary and at the foot of a 1220-metre mountain which is often snowcapped for several months of the year, is Australia's second oldest city. Compared with the mainland centres its rate of development has been slow and it retains in its commercial quarter and along the waterfront, many exceptionally fine stone buildings built in late Georgian and early Victorian times. They are numerous enough to contribute to the first impression it makes on newcomers. Here is an old, small, nineteenth century town, strongly maritime in flavour, whose citizens are proud enough of their history to preserve visual evidence of it. Hobart always appears freshly bathed, gay and, at the same time, relaxed. It is picturesque but never twee. Its citizens look as if they are very well aware that a half hour's drive in the family motor-car will take them to an apple orchard, a hopfield, a lonely beach, or the foot of a mountain crag. Of all Australian cities, Hobart fits the works of man more harmoniously into the pattern of nature.

By contrast, Adelaide seems to be gallantly — and successfully — defying the austere Outback which advances almost to its northern boundaries. It has a low rainfall — on an average only a little over 500 millimetres a year. It has desert skies — a clear, hard blue in winter, often hazed by dust in summer. Sprinklers, tossing out silvery water in endless loops, keep its cincture of parklands and playing fields bright green the year round. The flowers in its gardens are almost stridently bright. Its architecture, vaguely late-Victorian in the main commercial area, is entirely unobtrusive. Adelaide is *avante-garde* provincial, orderly, culture-conscious and joyously open-air in its setting between the bush-covered Mount Lofty Ranges and the placid waters of St Vincent's Gulf.

Two thousand kilometres away on the other side of the continent, Perth shares many of its characteristics — a site between mountains and sea, a warm, dry climate and space in which to expand.

The West Australian capital, however, is built on more undulating land and on the banks of the

Swan River where it broadens into the tidal Perth Water. Like Brisbane, its much less self-conscious and much more untidy sister in sub-tropical Queensland, it reflects river moods and, until recently when a great mining boom in the back country stirred long-dormant ambitions for economic stature, its pace was leisurely and its pleasures amiably rustic. One of Perth's greatest assets is a 400-hectare park on high land overlooking the centre of the city. The reserve was proclaimed in 1871 and its native bush has been carefully preserved and improved. Today it is one of the most delightful recreation reserves in the nation — a captivating show-window for the State's unique trees and wildflowers.

There are few inland cities of much size in Australia and fewer still in which an architectural awareness, visionary planning, or consistent civic pride have much contributed to the quality of living. Where they are favourably sited — as along the Murray Valley or the New England tablelands of northern New South Wales — they tend to be dull and utilitarian in appearance. No one in them seems ever to have been inspired by the idea of creating anything more beautiful and permanent than a run-of-the-mill public park, a Town Hall with a facade, a conventionally dreary stone church or, in this day and age, a Civic Centre with a small auditorium for theatrical and musical performances.

Nevertheless, these country towns can be extremely pleasant places to live in if one's main consideration is the enjoyment of rural pursuits. Many are set in a countryside of great natural beauty.

A few provincial cities, notably Ballarat and Bendigo in Victoria, Armidale in New South Wales and a scattering of industrial towns up the Queensland and New South Wales coasts, have an atmosphere of durability. The rest give an odd impression of impermanence even if their material prosperity is manifest in a plethora of petrol-filling stations and supermarkets. No doubt they are the modern equivalents of the frontier towns which grew up on the prairies of the United States a century ago.

The national capital, Canberra, is of course, the exception to the rule that many inland centres of population look like potential ghost towns. On Canberra Australians have fiercely concentrated their talents in an effort to prove that they are practical visionaries — that they can express the creative urge no less effectively in urban planning, development and improvement than in other fields of endeavour.

The result is striking. The governmental and administrative heart of the nation has been created to minute and long-considered specifications. A city of wide streets, sweeping boulevards, artificial lakes, fountains and aseptic architecture, has been implanted in a wide amphitheatre on the western slopes of the Australian Alps. Two million choice trees have been planted on public lands to soften the contours of concrete, brick and stone, bring gaiety to spring, cool shade to summer, decoration to autumn and dignity to winter.

Canberra is a mini-metropolis compounded of parks, gardens, plantations, neo-classical public buildings and standardised commercial premises and dwelling houses, all in precisely evaluated proportions. But sheer contrivance has achieved beauty — and expressed the conviction of Australians that they can always win for themselves, in their urban living, the best of two worlds.

over: Sydney's City Skyline and Harbour

This spectacular view of Sydney's modern skyline shows how far the city has spread. The many boats moored in the foreground on the North Shore give a clue to the Sydneysiders' lifestyle.
Set on a vast natural harbour and blessed with a pleasant climate, sailing, waterskiing and other water sports are very popular — and even travel to work can be more pleasant when it is by ferry or hydrofoil across the harbour.

above: Ruins of the Model Prison, Port Arthur, Tasmania

Built in 1830 by Governor Arthur to centralise Tasmania's penal establishment and provide a high security gaol, the notorious Model Prison housed more than 30 000 convicts under appallingly harsh conditions in the 37 years of its existence. The main buildings were sold to private interests after the settlement was abandoned in 1877, but most were destroyed or severely damaged by a disastrous bushfire in 1897.

above right: Constitution Dock, Hobart, Tasmania

The island State's capital is strongly maritime in character. The wharves of its busy river port accommodate passenger and cargo liners from all over the world and a myriad of smaller craft including pleasure yachts have berths or moorings by the Derwent's banks. Tasmanians are famed for their enthusiasm about sailing and boating.

right: National Gallery, Canberra

Imaginative planning and the skills of noted Australian architects have combined to make Australia's Federal Capital a city of grace and distinction, rich in parklands, plantations and immaculately tended public gardens. The now extensive and complex site has been ingeniously landscaped to take advantage of a superb setting in an amphitheatre of the Australian Alps.

above: Yarra River, Melbourne

Fine views of the city can always be obtained from the south bank of the river. Barbecues are dotted along the grassy banks and, at weekends, the more energetic can hire a bicycle and ride along a scenic riverside bicycle track. Melbourne is a metropolis of architectural inconsistencies. Yet it has dignity and beauty conferred by wide, tree-lined streets and avenues and spacious public gardens.

right: Tasman Bridge, Hobart

On the west bank of the lovely Derwent now spanned by a modern bridge with parkland approaches, Hobart is Australia's most southerly city. It retains much of its original architectural character, particularly on the waterfront where fine stone buildings of Georgian design have been jealously preserved against the incursion of commercial 'developers'.

over: Autumn, King George Terrace, Canberra

above left: Night Falls over Adelaide

A view from Mount Osmond. South Australia's capital is built on the narrow coastal plain between the Gulf of Saint Vincent and the abruptly rising Mount Lofty Ranges which command striking panoramas of the city. On a clear evening street lighting diffused by haze creates an exciting glow-worm cave effect.

left: Festival Centre, Adelaide

Situated on the curving banks of the Torrens River is the famous Festival Centre, hub of Adelaide's biennial festival. The city centre is completely surrounded by parklands, with beautiful flower beds, playgrounds and sports fields.

above: Metropolitan Brisbane

Straddling the winding, tidal Brisbane River 20 kilometres from its mouth, Brisbane is a sunny, easy-going city, favoured by a sub-tropical climate which is mild the year round and excellent for the cultivation of vivid ornamental trees such as poincianas, jacarandas and silky oaks. They flourish alongside deciduous exotics introduced from Europe and North America. Southern Queensland must be one of the few parts of the world where apples, pears and plums fruit in the home orchard alongside bananas and pawpaws.

above left: Crater Lakes, Mount Gambier, South Australia

Four deep and beautiful lakes in the crater of a long extinct volcano are the pride of Mount Gambier, largest town in South Australia's rich south east. The Blue Lake is 180 metres deep and has walls 80 metres high. Its waters have the mysterious property of changing colour between summer and winter. They are blue from November to March and slate grey from March to November.

left: Victorian Arts Centre, Melbourne

The imposing spire is part of the Victorian Arts Centre which also includes the National Gallery of Victoria, the Melbourne Concert Hall and three theatres. Melbourne's traditional position as the cultural and financial centre of the nation has been challenged by Sydney, but Melbourne still has an unruffled style and elegance all its own.

above: Spring in Canberra

More than two million native and exotic trees have been planted on public lands since the Federal Capital site was proclaimed in 1913. Many are flowering varieties which thrive in the cool climate and are at their best in spring when cherry, plum, peach and apple blossom transforms suburban streets.

Living Deserts
Of The Centre

Someone once wrote that Australia has a dead heart — that the greater part of its interior is red desert, a region of terrifying loneliness and perpetual thirst. The description has since been uncritically repeated by geography teachers all over the world.

It is a description which can be attributed only to an abysmally insensitive observer.

While it is true that roughly three million square kilometres of Australia's surface receive less than 250 millimetres of rain a year and that another three million square kilometres receive between 200 and 350 millimetres, only a small percentage of this is desert in the true sense of the word. There are few shifting sand dunes of the type which covers a large part of the Sahara and still fewer areas as totally devoid of plant and animal life as parts of Saudi Arabia, northern Chile, and Central Asia. On the contrary, the inland sustains such an abundance of specially adapted plant and animal life that some climatologists refuse to describe it as desert at all.

The Centre is made up of main types of terrain and soil — all components of the great shield of ancient sedimentary rocks which form about half the continent.

This shield is really a gigantic plateau which has been tilted by a gradual wrinkling of the earth's crust. Its western rim is exposed in a series of scarps bordering the Indian Ocean. The longest of these is the Darling Range in the south which rises to about 600 metres. Eminences twice that height occur in the north-west.

The plateau peters out 2500 kilometres to the east in the salt lake country and the Simpson Desert. The surface of Lake Eyre is actually 12 metres below sea level.

There is little or no surface water on this vast inclined plane except in a few rare localities where substantial springs rise to the surface. In summer it is lethally hot but it is far from lifeless and far from monotonous once one has become accustomed to its atmosphere of almost limitless spaciousness.

There are four main types of country in the Centre: compacted red sandhills which may retain their undulating contours or be flattened out into level plains with clayey subsoil; expanses of rock rubble and gibber (rounded nodules of ironstone which tend to increase in size as minerals held in solution are deposited by the evaporation of water drawn up to the surface); claypans thickly covered by glittering layers of salt and gypsum over which mirages dance throughout the day; and finally mountain ranges of tough rocks which have resisted the forces of erosion for millions of years.

Each type supports a distinctive vegetation (with the exception of the claypans which are quite naked) and distinctive forms of animal life. All, however, share a common characteristic. They have evolved to survive intense heat and prolonged drought.

In the sandy tracts the predominant plant species is the mulga (*Acacia aneura*), an incredibly tough little tree which can grow to a height of 10 metres but rarely exceeds 4 or 5. The foliage — tough, flattened phyllodes instead of leaves — is a sombre, bluish green and the root system is enormous. Mallee gums compete with mulga in southern latitudes where the silvery leafed bluebush and the much more common saltbush provide partial ground cover. The former indicates the presence of a limy subsoil and the latter the accumulation of saline water just below the surface. Both species are important sources of food for stock and native animals.

Stony tracts and true gibber plains support a less varied flora but they are often covered, in whole or in part, by spinifex (*Triodia*) the most widely distributed of the desert grasses.

Spinifex grows in round, pincushion-like clumps a couple of metres across when the plant is mature. For most of the year it is pale gold or neutral in tint but after rain puts out bright green shoots and russet flower heads. Like saltbush, bluebush and smaller desert succulents, spinifex is important to the ecology of the gibber country. It provides food and shelter for innumerable small marsupials, reptiles, birds and insects. The Aborigines of the north-west used to harvest its seed for flour — and find many a succulent titbit for roasting in its thorny depths.

Fascinating and full of life though the plains of the Inland are, the true beauty of Australia's living heart is concentrated in the high country.

The mountains of Central Australia are entirely different in character from those of the Great Divide and the western escarpment. Few large

left: Organ Pipes Bluff, Finke River,
Northern Territory

trees grow on them. Only rarely does water flow through the sunless canyons with which they are cleft. Their appeal lies in the play of the sun's light on exposed rock faces etched into intricate patterns by wind and temperature fluctuations and often brightly stained by mineral leaching.

The best known of the desert ranges are the Macdonnells and the Musgraves, most easily reached from Alice Springs, a town to which the air and motor age has brought great prosperity. Tourists from all over the world flock to it to enjoy the magnificent winter climate and admire the painted gorges and monstrous tors and boulders of the surrounding countryside.

Some 400 kilometres to the south-west, off the end of the Petermann Range is the world's largest monolith, Ayers Rock — a stupendous mass of conglomerate with a circumference of nearly 10 kilometres. The summit is 850 metres above sea level and it is ringed by 335-metre cliffs which reflect an unbelievable range of intense colour when the sun is low in the sky, or at midday when it appears as a flattened golden dome thrusting against the fine blue-enamel sky. Quite justifiably it ranks as one of the scenic wonders of the world.

The nearby Mutiguluna waterhole attracts much wildlife including herds of red kangaroos and emus and the sides of the rock itself are riddled with caves adorned with Aboriginal paintings that tell the story of mythical ancestors in the 'dreaming time' when the world was created. These galleries are of absorbing interest to anthropologists. They are of great antiquity and unfortunately are now fading fast.

People who visit Ayers Rock usually continue their journey another 30 kilometres to view The Olgas, a group of somewhat less overpowering monoliths which from certain aspects resemble enormously magnified pebbles.

In the Pilbara division of Western Australia are several sizeable desert ranges which rival those of the Centre in brilliant colouring. In the Hamersleys, where in recent years large iron mines have been opened up, the rock tones range from blue-black and rich chocolate through magenta and crimson to pale cadmium yellow. The famous red gorges near the Wittenoom settlement south of Port Hedland are now regular stopover points on the tourist bus routes. They are strikingly, almost garishly beautiful but they do not in my opinion

match the Isabella and Gregory Ranges east of Marble Bar, a ghost town which claims the dubious distinction of recording the highest summer temperatures of any inhabited place in Australia.

The quintessence of everthing scenically arresting in the Outback will be found among the scattering of blood-red mesas and sweeping spinifex valleys along the western fringe of the Great Sandy Desert.

This country receives less than 200 millimetres of rainfall a year — and most of that falls in violent thunderstorms sweeping in from the Indian Ocean — but it swarms with life. The Oakover and De Grey Rivers which drain a vast area of sand plain inland follow the habit of all north-western streams. They flow underground beneath dry spits and shingle beds for most of their length — except in the cyclone season — but here and there rise to the surface in the form of clear, green pools that may be anything from a hundred metres to a few kilometres long. An astounding diversity of bird and animal life congregates at these watering places.

It would be hard to imagine a more delightful camping place for a naturalist than a site beside one of the deep reaches in the Carrawine Gorge or on the banks of the Nullagine River just above its junction with the De Grey. Ancient river gums, casuarinas and wattles border the waterholes which are far less turbid than most found in the inland and their surfaces reflect the mirror image of delicately textured foliage and the bright hues and bold outlines of gorge rims where the floods of bygone ages have cut a way through the rocky ribs of the plain.

In winter this whole region is the Outback of romance — a land of drenching sunshine, limitless vistas, vast silences and cold, star-burdened nights. Then, when spring approaches, the rock-pools in the desert start to shrink and the wild life of the *pindan* start to move in to the permanent water — euros, wallabies, bandicoots and tiny, pouched mice; dingoes, feral cats, and scrubber cattle descended from many generations of cleanskins — even, occasionally, wild donkeys and camels which have crossed the desert from the Kimberley country to the north-east where they have reached pest proportions.

Dusk is peak traffic period for myriads of birds coming in to drink after a day's foraging in the spinifex — pink and grey galahs, sulphur crested cockatoos, budgerigars, wrens and zebra finches, honey eaters and bronzewing and crested pigeons in platoons. Then, as darkness falls the flying-fox colonies in the rock clefts bestir themselves and flap away squeaking to join the other mammals going on night-shift at food gathering.

Sometimes after a rainstorm or a series of unusually heavy dews has moistened the soil to the depth of a few millimetres, the pindan bursts into flower. Sturt's desert pea and desert rose run like wildfire over the flats. Sandhills are suddenly clothed with white and yellow everlasting daisies and pink mulla-mulla. Parakeelya, wild cockscomb, Star of Bethlehem and potato-bush blaze in the depressions to which moisture has gravitated. The spinifex puts out new green thorns and henna flower heads and dwarf banksias and hakeas bear tiny balls and cylinders of cream, lemon and scarlet.

At such times if you look closely on the shady side of the sand ripples you may be lucky enough to witness the miraculous resurrection of the small desert ephemerals — plants of minute and perhaps unclassified genera which germinate, grow, flower, seed and die in a matter of days. They are the most delicate, transient and brilliant things in floral nature.

Minor desert ranges like the Isabellas and the Gregorys, and the permanent waterholes, are refugees from drought for a bewildering variety of living things — sources from which the fauna and flora of hundreds of thousands of square kilometres is regenerated after a run of rainless years has taken toll.

After days of travelling over flat country it is almost unbearably exciting to come within sight of low, purple mountains on the horizon and to observe how the whole mood of nature changes as one approaches them. They are always full of surprises — perhaps a small, hidden valley of waving golden grass ringed by ridges where the magnificent white trunks of ghost gums (*Eucalyptus papuana*) are silhouetted against the sky; or pandanus groves or grottoes where tiny ferns and mintbush grows; or rocky tors from which a mighty panorama of cinnabar plain is unexpectedly revealed.

Every hour of the day in this country has its own colour signature. At dawn the peaks are painted in flaming orange. At noon they are red and purple. By late afternoon they are saxe-blue and gold. And when the afterglow of sunset has faded they are velvety black.

Here in the deep silence of night, broken only by the occasional stirrings of roosting birds and the stealthy comings and goings of nocturnal animals, the traveller comes close to a comprehension of the mysterious beginnings of things — the dreaming time of man's creation when perception of the world's beauty invested him with a soul.

above: Sunrise on Malu Rocks, The Olgas, Northern Territory

A group of gargantuan sandstone 'boulders' 30 kilometres west of Ayer's Rock at the geographical centre of the continent, the Olgas rise from an arid plain clothed in stunted mulga and spinifex. Like all Central Australian mountains, their vivid colours change dramatically as the light varies. The rich gold of early morning may have taken on a crimson tint by midday or been transformed to deep purple by nightfall.

right: Ayers Rock, Northern Territory

The world's greatest monolith lies 400 kilometres south-west of Alice Springs. The Rock has a circumference of nearly 10 kilometres and rises to a height of 348 metres above its base. Rightly classed as one of the scenic wonders of the world.

above: Termite 'City', near Hall's Creek, Western Australia

White ants — or, more accurately, termites — construct these extraordinary mounds of digested mud which are a feature of northern landscapes, particularly in the Northern Territory and the Kimberleys. The hills may be 3 to 4 metres high and contain a labyrinth of galleries in which the destructive creatures store food, and shelter from the heat. Large areas of the flat, dry country between Fitzroy Crossing and Halls Creek are covered by these bizarre colonies.

right: Hanks Head Lookout, Murchison River, Western Australia

The stony Darling escarpment north of Geraldton is split by Murchison River in a series of wild, red-walled gorges which are overpowering in the atmosphere of barren savagery that hangs over them. This is country for the nature lover who likes his scenery raw and strong flavoured. Only a few miles away there are lush wheatlands and a coast notable for its gentle, pleasant contours.

above left: Cattle Mustering in the Pindan, Western Australia

Aboriginal stockmen are the backbone of the cattle industry in Northern Australia. They are born horsemen and know the Big Sky country where their nomadic ancestors hunted food in the days before the white men came with their flocks and herds to graze — and often kill out — the desert pasture plants. Most of the pindan is now badly eroded by over-grazing but it retains its unique, almost terrifying beauty.

left: Hamersley Range from the air, Western Australia

Stretching for nearly 500 kilometres across the arid Pilbara division of the far North West, the Hamersleys are noted for the wide variety of colours reflected from their rocks. The entire region is highly mineralised and many of the mountains are composed of high grade iron ore which is now being mined extensively for export to Japan.

above: The Devil's Marbles near Wauchope, Northern Territory

This aptly named group of gigantic boulders is located beside the Stuart Highway about 100 kilometres south of Tennant Creek between Alice Springs and Darwin. Many such rocks lie on the surface of Centralian deserts, but few are so symmetrically weathered or so accessible to sightseers.

over: Carr Boyd Range, East Kimberley, Western Australia

103

above: Mount Sonder, Macdonnell Range, Northern Territory

Due west of Alice Springs, Sonder is one of the giants of the Centre, rising to a height of 1346 metres above sea level. The rock of which it is formed is estimated to be 400 million years old. It is slashed by deep gorges and its original bedding planes have been so twisted by pressures in the earth's crust that they point vertically to the sky. Straggling lines of river gums at the foot of the massif indicate the courses of underground streams.

right: Palm Valley, Northern Territory

Rare and graceful Livingstonia palms (*L. mariae*) thrive in this lush oasis 118 kilometres south of the famous Hermannsburg Aboriginal Mission. The species grows to a height of about 18 metres. Their nearest relatives are nearly 1600 kilometres away on the Fortesque River in Western Australia — a fact which supports the theory advanced by some scientists that the climate of the Centre has been arid only in comparatively recent times. They argue that many of the plants of today's deserts are drought resistant descendents of genera which evolved in a wet, tropical climate.

above: Narrow-leafed Parakeelya, Northern Territory

One of the most widely distributed of the desert succulents, *Calendrinia vemota* carpets enormous areas of the plains after rain. These days it is regarded mainly as decorative, but 80 or 90 years ago the pioneers of the Never Never considered it a blessing because camels on which they depended for transport grazed it avidly.

right: Gorge near Wittenoom, Western Australia

Rich red, violet and deep brown are typical rock colours in the Hamersley Ranges. They are especially intense after rain has washed away the powdery ironstone dust which normally covers them.

left: Standley Chasm, Northern Territory

The cliffs are 76 metres high, their bases only 4 to 6 metres apart.

Viking O'Neil
Penguin Books Australia Ltd
487 Maroondah Highway, PO Box 257
Ringwood, Victoria 3134, Australia
Penguin Books Ltd
Harmondsworth, Middlesex, England
Penguin Books
40 West 23rd Street, New York, N.Y. 10010, U.S.A.
Penguin Books Canada Limited
2801 John Street, Markham, Ontario, Canada L3R 1B4
Penguin Books (N.Z.) Ltd
182-190 Wairau Road, Auckland 10, New Zealand

First published by Lloyd O'Neil Pty Ltd 1970
Reprinted 1982, 1986
This edition published by Penguin Books Australia Ltd 1987
Copyright © Robin Smith, 1970

Produced by Viking O'Neil
56 Claremont Street, South Yarra, Victoria 3141, Australia
A division of Penguin Books Australia Ltd

Printed and bound in Hong Kong through Bookbuilders Ltd

National Library of Australia
Cataloguing-in-Publication data

Smith, Robin (Robin Vaughan Francis).
   The beauty of Australia.

ISBN 0 670 90022 2.

1. Australia — Description and travel — 1976-
Views. I. White, Osmar, 1909-   . I. Title.

994.06'3'0222